GRAVES'
GARDEN
BIRDS

GEORGE GRAVES

Selected British Garden Birds

β

PARSIMONY PRESS

MM

First published in the United Kingdom in 2000
Second impression 2000
Parsimony Press Ltd
West Huntspill, Somerset

A CIP catalogue record for this book is available from the
British Library

ISBN 1 902979 08 7

Little Owl woodcut on title page, Thomas Bewick 1797
Engravings by George Graves 1811 and 1813
Photography by Stephen Lovell-Davis
Typesetting by Norton/Russell Enterprises
Colour reproduction by Articolour, Italy
Printed by LEGO SpA, Italy

Foreword

'Why do you use these old pictures in a book about birds when there are so many good photographs you could use instead?' you may ask.

There are several reasons. There have always been bird fanciers. Today we have enthusiasts like Bill Oddie. But it was in the 3rd century BC that Zenodotus wrote of the aggressive determination with which robins try for a large territory, 'One bush does not hold two robins'. George Graves was born in the 18th century, and published his first book of 48 British birds in 1811. The second book came out in 1813, and these two lasted for more than ten years before the third volume came out. For that reason the third is rather hard to find.

There were more famous ornithologists. There are more complete sets. But the love he had for his birds, and the vigour with which they were shown, so beautifully engraved and coloured, do make his books worth preserving.

And that is another reason. Books of such quality are getting harder and harder to find. Not only do they get lost and deteriorate, but they are too often vandalised.

The world is unfortunately filled with people who buy these books; chop them up and frame the contents for the sake of making more money than they deserve. At least if you want to chop *these* up and frame them you are not destroying one of the few copies of a book that has been protected for two hundred years.

We have kept the Latin names true to Graves. You will occasionally see something different in brackets, this being the name preferred by modern-day ornithologists.

There are many more birds that you are likely to see in or around a garden than these few here. Yet many birds that were common in the early nineteenth century can no longer be seen at all in Britain. Even in your lifetime you may have noticed how birds like sparrows are no longer a sure visitor to the table outside a pub where you are having a sandwich.

You have, we hope, a mini-feast in store, but no sparrow this time.

The Birds

STRIX FLAMMEA
(TYTO ALBA)

White or Barn Owl

Feathers surrounding the eyes are intermixed with hairs; the body hairs are very soft and on the underside have two shafts coming from the same quill; legs feathered to the toes, very strong and the middle claw is serrated.

With a wingspan of nearly a yard, and over a foot long, it weighs four times as much as the little owl. At night they look ghostly white, and have always been welcomed by the farmers in whose buildings they so often nest.

Mice are what they eat most of, and Gilbert White once clocked a pair of them as they hunted in the hour before sunset in summer. One or the other returned with a mouse in its claws every five minutes, which is good going, since mice do their best to avoid being caught. He was also pleased to see the tricks they got up to in order to extract the mouse from their claws so that they could use their feet to get under the eaves into the nest.

Great Titmouse

Bill compressed, straight, short, and sharp pointed;
nostrils round, covered with vibrissae*; tongue laciniated,
points terminating nearly on a line; toes separate, hind one
the longest.

Perhaps people once had a puritanical dislike of
calling this the Great Tit. Now the nicer Titmouse
has almost disappeared from the ornithological
vocabulary.

This bird, like the blue tit, is smart as a wagonload
of monkeys, and you can give yourself a lot of
entertainment by setting it tasks to get the winter
food you leave it. Since so few people have milk
delivered, thus denying them the drink they so
enjoyed on your doorstep, they have had to look for
other ways of thieving. The beautifully illustrated
AA/Reader's Digest Book of British Birds describes
one great tit hauling up a thread, loop by loop, using
its foot to hold the loops until the nut attached to the
end was in reach.

They are also vigorous in defence of their fledglings,
and have been known even to attack magpies, which
is not bad for three quarters of an ounce against
nine ounces.

*New word = nostril hairs

PARUS CŒRULEUS
(PARUS CÆRULEUS)

Blue Titmouse

Bill strong, sharp pointed, very thick at the base; legs slender; toes divided at the base, the hinder claw very long. The female has duller colours.

It is little more than four inches long, weighing five and a half drams or a third of an ounce.

This is a pretty bird with the same generic characteristics as the Great Tit. As it feeds mainly on small insects it can be unpopular with fruit farmers since it destroys many buds for the sake of a snack of eggs or larvae.

Blue tits are used by sadistic ornithologists to take tests, and have shown an extraordinary ability to overcome all sorts of mechanical barriers, pegs or drawers, to get at food. It was they who apparently taught other tits to pierce the tops of milk bottles.

They are as vigorous in defending their fledglings against magpies as any of their cousins, and since they will also be first to go to a nut dispenser you will have plenty of opportunity of looking at them in the cold months.

CORVUS GLANDARIUS
(GARRULUS GLANDARIUS)

Jay

Bill strong; the upper mandible has a notch near the tip which is much hooked; feathers on the forehead and crown long and capable of being erected; legs and claws strong, the edges of the latter are very sharp and project beyond the under surface.

This most colourful of the crow family is about fourteen inches long with a wingspan of twenty-one inches, half as much again, and it weighs about six ounces. Although the colours are the same the female is a bit smaller and weighs maybe an ounce less.

It builds its nest in low trees, of twigs lined with moss and grass. Its call is as unpleasant as that of the magpie, although it does have more conversation, and it tends to spend more time in the woods than the magpie. Because it mainly eats grain, fruit and the seeds of most kinds of forest trees it is nearly as unpopular with farmers as is the magpie. But, unlike the magpie, it spends less time raiding the eggs and chicks of other birds.

CORVUS PICA
(PICA PICA)

Magpie

*The female, a little smaller, has the same colour as
the male, with a slightly shorter tail. They seem black
and white, but the black can in fact reflect as a whole
range of different colours.*

It is nearly eighteen inches long and weighs
about nine ounces.

It is one of the few birds that is shot, not for
eating but merely to make one less magpie.
Especially in spring, their destructive ability is
immense. They will eat unhatched eggs, using
every wile to get the sitting bird off the nest.
Then, later, they will eat the fledglings.

As Graves points out, the magpie will eat any
kind of meat whether fresh or putrid. 'It will
attack young lambs and weakly sheep, the eyes
of the latter it first assails and mostly succeeds
if the animal is incapable of rising.'

They may look handsome, if a bit funereal; but
there are too many of them.

Green Woodpecker

*Bill two and a half inches long, tip wedge-shaped
and very hard; tongue nearly eight inches long,
covered with thick gluten, capable of retaining small
insects.*

The bird is thirteen inches long, so that the
tongue is more than half as long as the bird. The
wingspan is eighteen inches, and the weight is
about six ounces.

They are more often heard than seen, and on the
whole they are a good friend to have in the
garden, since most of what they like to eat isn't
much good for what you might be growing.

Beekeepers have been known to complain that
they bang away at hives in an effort to get at the
grubs, and sometimes they go for fruit. But
insects are what they really like, particularly
ants.

We wonder how much the tongue weighs.

ALCEDO ISPIDA
(ALCEDO ATTHIS)

Common Kingfisher

Bill long, straight, thick at the base, sharp pointed; tongue entire, broad, pointed, very short; legs very short; toes. three forward, one backward, the three lower joints connected by a strong membrane; middle toe serrated on the underside.

Its length is seven inches and its wingspan eleven.

Owing, says Graves, to the disproportion of the head, which, with the bill, is nearly half of the whole length, the bird appears very clumsy. He goes on to say that 'it can be observed to sit for hours on a stone or stump by the banks of running streams observing the movements of small fish, which, the instant they approach, it darts on with amazing velocity, and will remain some seconds under water securing. It brings its prey alive to land, and beats it to death before swallowing.'

Alas, nowadays these most beautiful birds are rarer, more timid and harder to see. Only the most patient, or the most lucky, get the pleasure.

It is extraordinary that this lovely bird, which really belongs in the warm climate of India, has managed to survive here at all.

Missel Thrush

Bill straight, the upper mandible slightly curves towards
the point, and in some species has a notch towards the tip.
Mouth furnished at the sides with a number of stiffish
bristles. Tongue jagged at the tip. Nostrils naked. Toes,
three forward, one backward, the middle one connected to
the outer as far as the first joint.

It is eleven inches with a wingspan of eighteen
inches, weighing around five ounces.

In *The Natural History of Selborne*, Gilbert White
remarks on how vigorously these birds will defend
their territory against magpies and jays, and that on
one occasion it took a several magpies to overcome
the mother before they could eat the young.

Browning talks of 'That's the wise thrush: he sings
each song twice over, lest you should think he never
could recapture the first fine careless rapture.'

It is a glorious song, and can be heard from January
until, as Graves' friend Mr Montague pointed out,
'the temperature sinks below forty-five degrees'.
This, we regret to say, is now called seven Celsius.

Bulfinch

Bill short, very strong, the upper mandible is much hooked and is very sharp pointed; eyes large and black; legs slender; claws long and curved.

The bulfinch is six inches long, has a wingspan of about ten inches and weighs nearly three quarters of an ounce.

This has always been an unpopular bird in gardens and orchards, since it feeds on the flower buds of most kinds of fruit trees. It has been clocked at 30 a minute, which is a deal faster than anybody can even pick the fruit that manages to survive. In winter the damage it causes is less, since it seems to like most winter berries, especially hawthorn and privet (and the less privet we see the better!)

It is thought that they mate for life, but we don't know whether this shows a commendable constancy or a disinclination to have to go through all that courting again every spring.

In our passion for keeping the manufacturers of printers ink eating, a second *l* has now been added to make it 'bullfinch'.

Yellow Bunting

Bill strong; incurved edges very sharp; the knob in the roof of the upper mandible very prominent; tongue is bifid and has a few fine hairs at its extreme points.

It is six and a half inches long, and ten inches wide and weighs about an ounce. It is also known as a yellowhammer, and in the days when we had hedgerows it was plentiful. It built its nest low down, mostly of farmyard waste, like straw, and in winter it grew fat on the spilled grain that was so easily available in the quantities needed by a one ounce bird. It was plentiful enough to be eaten, like the lark, to which it was said to be 'quite equal in flavour'. Yet it has still managed to survive.

We tend to try to give words to some birdsong. This little friend's is described as 'a-little-bit-of-bread-and-no-cheese'. In Scotland they say it is something different, 'the deil-deil-deil take ye'.

FRINGILLA CARDUELIS
(CARDUELIS CARDUELIS)

Goldfinch

Bill conic; legs slender; colours nearly similar in both sexes, though the wing coverts are inclined to brown.

We know it is nearly five inches long, but have not been able to weigh one. It also makes a lovely nest, made of moss, dried grass and lichens, and lined with the down of thistles, hair and wool.

The popularity of this bird has maybe done many of them few favours. It doesn't attack fruit trees, for its preferred food is the seeds of thistles and teasels, and the leaves of groundsel. For the first few weeks, the young are also fed on caterpillars. Nowadays this may be more of a pity as one of its favourites was the caterpillar of the peacock butterfly, which they would find among the nettles.

Because of its beauty and its benign attitude to diet it was much used as a cagebird as an alternative to a canary, with whom it would happily breed. In confinement its appearance often changed; most usually it became black, but occasionally completely white. It seems that those fed only on hemp seed became quite black.

Common Wagtail

Bill slender, very soft and slightly notched near the end;
tongue fringed at the tip; legs slender; toes, three forward,
one behind, the centre one connected to the outer one as far
as the first joint; the hind toe and claw long; tail very long.

It is about seven and a half inches long, with a
wingspan of ten and a half inches and weighs about
three quarters of an ounce. It is now known as the
Pied Wagtail.

Graves said that 'this bird is too well known to
require further description'. But he did point out
that in winter they lose the black on the throat and
chin, which become white. This was for some time
thought to be another variety.

They usually build their nest among stones, made of
moss and dry fibres and even wool, and because their
eggs are like those of the cuckoo these nests become
a target, despite the vigour with which they try to
drive the cuckoo away. The wagtail likes to be near
ponds and streams where there are more insects,
and it jumps up at them as they fly near.

Worth watching.

Robin

*It is about five and a half inches long with a wingspan
of eight and a half inches and it weighs a little over half
an ounce.*

It was known in Graves' time as the Redbreast. Now
this is less common. It is also called Erithacus
rubecula.

Whatever its name it is a disagreeable bird. In 1961
it was chosen as Britain's national bird, perhaps
by people who thought of Britain as 'Perfidious
Albion'.

No garden bird is as adept as the robin at
ingratiating itself with the humans who own the
garden it has chosen as its territory, sitting perkily
on the handle of the spade waiting for worms. Yet it
is unbelievably beastly to any other robin that has
the temerity to want to get close to its trough.
Robins do not hesitate to kill other robins.

Happily, their hypocritical and aggressive lives last,
for most of them, only a little more than a year.

Common Wren

*Bill nearly half an inch long, slightly curved; eyes large
and dark; claws large in proportion to size.*

It weighs just over a quarter of an ounce (the weight
of a grape) and is three and three quarters of an inch
long.

This little bird is irresistibly loveable. Only the
goldcrest, which weighs 70 grains, is smaller. As
there are 7000 grains to the pound, you would get
100 goldcrests or about 60 wrens to the pound.

It doesn't migrate and it builds its nest mostly where
it can find a little hole. The male builds several,
giving the female a choice. But when the weather
gets colder they may all pile in together to keep
warm. Ten, it is said, were once found in a coconut
shell.

They use what materials are available for their nest,
and they live on insects, seldom making more than
short flights, well protected from larger predatory
birds by their camouflage colouring.

They are worth helping in winter since they don't
carry enough fat to fry a pea.

Chimney Swallow

Bill short, broad at base, tip curving; nostrils open; tongue short, broad, bifid; tail forked; toes, three before, one behind; legs very slender; colours alike in both sexes.

It is seven to eight inches long, a little over a foot in wingspan. It weighs about half an ounce.

Few birds are better known, since they always attach themselves to human dwellings. Pairs tend to come back to the same place each year. We had one pair that nested for two years in a pruning hook resting on nails in the potting shed.

Regrettably, they are now less common, falling as they do to pollution and the determination of hunters waiting between Britain and Africa.

Ring Pheasant

*Bill short, strong, convex; nostrils covered by an
arched process; sides of the head covered with bare
granulated skin; legs strong, usually furnished with a
spur on the inside; toes connected at their base with a
strong membrane.*

Unlike the finches, this bird will run up to about
three pounds in weight. Because it is bred and
fed for shooting, this imported bird has
gradually adapted to a less agreeable climate
than that from which it originally came.

It has become very common at the roadside,
where it often ends it life being hit by a car. Nor
is it uncommon in the garden, where there is
seldom either the equipment or the inclination
to kill it. Because it is considered more sporting
to shoot high-flying birds it is perhaps even
possible that the gene pool is being depleted of
the best pheasants and we may end up with
birds that never fly at all, when, so long as they
stand still, only Frenchmen will shoot them.

ARDEA MAJOR
(ARDEA CINEREA)

Common Heron

Bill straight, compressed, strong and sharp pointed, six inches long; nostrils linear; tongue sharp pointed; eyes large and piercing surrounded by bare skin; toes, three forward connected by a membrane to the first joint, the middle one pectinated, the hinder toe one-third shorter than the front ones.

This is as large a bird as you will find in this little book, being more than three feet long, with a wingspan of more than five feet. At three and a half pounds it weighs more than 400 tree creepers.

The heron used to be seen only near rivers and estuaries, but now it comes inland, perhaps in the hope of a goldfish waiting unsuspecting in some garden pond. We see a lot of them nowadays, sailing in stately splendour on slow-flapping wings, their legs trailing behind them just clearing the treetops in their leisurely flight. A handsome bird, and courteous enough to avoid those ponds that are sheltered by some fibreglass imitation heron.

Ah, yes. A new word. Pectinated is 'toothed like a comb'.

Tawny Owl

Bill strong, an inch and a quarter long, much hooked; legs strong, covered with feathers to the toes; claws sharp and strong, when the foot is distended, it covers a space nearly three inches square; tail composed of twelve feathers.

Female is larger, being seventeen inches long with a wingspan of nearly three feet and weighing nineteen ounces.

Phlegmatic, this one, as birds go. Like most owls it looks for its meals at night, and during the day it roosts more or less where it likes, where it is often mobbed by smaller birds without being much troubled or much inclined to move.

As part of its phlegmatic nature it has arranged its genes so that it can keep an eye out for potential danger by turning its head without having to go to the trouble of moving its body. Nor is it very picky about where it makes its nest, often using those of other birds, holes in trees or burrows in the ground to save itself the trouble of any unnecessary work in home-making. You are more likely to hear it than see it. A dialogue between two birds has one hooting, and the other doing what is normally described as 'Kee-wick'.

The Tawny Owl is not much like Owl in Winnie The Pooh. It is clearly Eeyore.

Little Owl

*Bill broad at the base and much curved, surrounded
with hair-like feathers which project beyond the bill;
legs feathered to the toes, which are covered with
down interspersed with hairs.*

The little owl has a wingspan of about fourteen
inches and a length of nine. It weighs about two
and a half ounces, which isn't much for this
amount of bird. The female is usually larger
than the male.

They say it only came to Britain from Europe
towards the end of Queen Victoria's reign, and
earned immediate unpopularity, since it spread
very vigorously, and was thought to live entirely
on pheasant chicks when they were available.

Both views are rubbish, since Graves had
included it in his book before Victoria was born,
and although it can be seen flying during the
day, it mostly hunts its food in the evening dusk,
and mainly has to put up with insects to keep
body and soul together.

PARUS CAUDATUS
(AEGITHALOS CAUDATUS)

Long-tailed Titmouse

Bill very short; feathers on the head and cheeks, rough; legs and claws strong; tail very long, the second feathers from the centre being three and a half inches long.

Five and a half inches long, six and a half wide, weighing nearly four drams.

Like the woodpecker, whose tongue is more than half as long as its body, this little bird's length is mostly tail. It is by no means the commonest of tits, as you will soon discover if you have a feeder, but it is worth encouraging if you have one around, if only for its elegance.

It also brings you another treat, a beautifully made nest, dome-shaped, looking like nothing so much as a vertical hedgehog, which they get into from the top. For this nest the bird is known in some places as the bottle tit, whereas in towns it is the ability of all tits to get into milk bottles that brings the association.

Common Cuckoo

Bill curved; tongue short; tail composed of ten flexible feathers; toes, two forwards and two backwards.

It is fifteen inches long with a twenty-five inch wingspan, and weighs four and a half ounces.

In the 19th century the cuckoo would commonly use a hedge-sparrow or ' dunnock' to foster its young and (if they can find one) this is still true today. It was Mr Genner who first recorded this phenomenon which you have probably seen in a wild-life film. There is this hairless fledgling, pushing either egg or fledgling – whatever it finds in the nest when it is itself hatched – using its back and elbows to roll its victim to the top of the nest and then with one final jerk slinging it out.

Its call may be a welcome harbinger of spring, but we would like it more if it wasn't brought up at the expense of its foster parents' chicks.

PICUS MAJOR
(DENDROCOPOS MAJOR)

Greater-spotted Woodpecker

Bill very strong, an inch and a quarter long; legs and claws strong; colours of the sexes alike except the female is black on the upper part of the head.

Length nine inches, wingspan fifteen and weighing about three ounces.

Now it is known as 'Great', for although it is half the size of the Green it is larger than the Lesser Spotted Woodpecker, which is small enough to make it hard to distinguish as it looks for its lunch.

The Greater Spotted, on the other hand, shows black and white bars on the underside of its wings, making it easier to recognise when it is flying.

It lays its snow-white eggs and rears its young in the hollow of a decayed tree. It finds the site by banging away until it hears a hollow sound, and then pecks out a tunnel which may be as much as two feet long.

No nonsense about making a nest. Once the entrance is made, the soft wood is all the comfort the chicks will get. It mostly feeds its young on caterpillars. Good for vegetable farmers, bad for butterflies.

Starling

Bill straight; tongue cleft; legs strong, covered with a few large scales; toes, three forward one backward, the centre connected to the outer one as far as the first joint.

You see these birds most often wheeling in enormous flocks silhouetted against the evening sky. City councils find them a pain, and, like the passenger pigeon, now extinct in the States, they can damage trees by their sheer weight of numbers, more than a branch can support.

In smaller quantities they are more agreeable, even tame. I remember being regarded, even inspected, with polite curiosity by a few of them when I was once sitting by the sea at Southwold.

LOXIA COCCOTHRAUSTES
(COCCOTHRAUSTES COCCOTHRAUSTES)

Haw-grosbeak

The bill is three quarters of an inch long, and unusually strong, being half an inch thick at its base; the points of most of the quill feathers are truncated, the tips of the first four or five are bent, somewhat in the form of an ancient battle-axe; legs slender, claws strong.

Weighing in at a little over two ounces, it is still seven inches long and has a wingspan of thirteen inches.

Now it is known as the Hawfinch, but its original name is better since it loves haw berries and it has a beak that is extraordinary. It can crack almost any kernel that the British woodland can offer it, and can munch its way through the berries of a privet hedge with equal enthusiasm. Here is a bird that weighs the merest whisper but has no difficulty cracking a cherry stone, a job that *you* would find hard with a pair of nutcrackers.

Chaffinch

The female is rather smaller and weighs two drams less than a male. Her colours are considerably duller.

Five inches long, nine inches wingspan. It weighs nearly one ounce.

Happily this is still a common bird, probably because it is such an omnivorous eater. From the setting of fruit until its ripening the chaffinch makes severe depredations on the cherry farmer's crop. But, on the other hand, while it is feeding its young in spring it uses an enormous number of caterpillars and small insects, thus compensating for what it deprives us of, off the trees.

It makes lovely nests, usually using materials that camouflage it against the surroundings, while still being 'a masterpiece of elegance and neatness'. In many areas the sexes separate, the females tending to go South while the more robust males put up with the Northern winters. Gilbert White points out that females often gather in enormous flocks.

Now it's called 'cœlebs' because ornithologists don't necessarily know their Latin.

Yellow Wagtail

The bill of this bird is like that of the Common Wagtail, but it is altogether a little smaller and its hind claw is nearly straight, not just longer than the front ones, but nearly twice as long.

The bird is about seven inches long with a nine and a half inch wingspan. It arrives in Britain in the latter half of March, and in 'elegance of shape, delicacy of colour and liveliness of manners, this bird is perhaps unequalled'.

It is sometimes confused with the Grey Wagtail, but it flies quicker than the Grey and with less undulation than the Common. It tends to feed in drier places than the Common Wagtail. It finds plenty of insects around farm animals and has been seen taking a fly off the nose of a cow or horse, while in cold damp weather it will eat the worms that have been roused to the surface by the trampling of cattle.

Known in some parts as the Yellow Dishwasher, it heads for warmer countries by the middle of October, leaving the Grey and the Common behind.

Redstart

Bill short; legs and claws slender; the female is light brown where the male is grey, and the other colours are less flamboyant than those of the male.

About six inches long with a wingspan of eight and a half inches; weighing a little over half an ounce.

The tail tends to look redder than it does in this picture, and is in fact how it got its name, *steart* being an early word for the tail. It arrives in the second half of April and leaves in the second half of September.

It is a great little singer, starting as soon as it arrives and continuing, often even at night, until the eggs are hatched. During most of June, until the fledglings leave the nest at the end of the month, it stops singing. Probably with regret.

Wood Pigeon

Bill weak and slender; nostril placed in a soft
protuberance that covers the base of the bill; tongue entire;
toes divided to their origin.

It is eighteen inches long with a wingspan of
twenty-nine inches and its usual weight is nearly
twenty ounces, about the same as a Tawny Owl.

To Graves and his contemporaries this was a Ring-
Dove or a Ring-Pigeon.

To those of us who were born before the Second
World War it was lunch. During the War it became
lunch that didn't use up any ration coupons.

Since the War it has become a widespread scavenger.
Farmers hate them, but don't seem to eat them very
much. You see them everywhere. You hear them
everywhere. And children can often perplex them by
cupping hands together and imitating the call, two
long hoots and a couple of short ones. Most grown-
ups have lost the knack.

The pigeons, therefore, probably regard us as stupid
and inarticulate. But convenient.